Live the Life You Love

EMPOWERING WOMEN THROUGH FRANCHISE OWNERSHIP

By LINDA SCHAEFFER

Live the Life You Love

©2024 by Linda Schaeffer

This book is lovingly dedicated to my family.

This book is lovingly dedicated to my family.

To my husband Scott, thank you for always supporting me and celebrating my success.

To my children Kevin (Daisey), Samantha (Zach), and Matt, you are my greatest treasures and constant sources of motivation. As I embarked on the journey of starting my first franchise, it was with the intention of creating a life where I could be both present for you and fulfilled in my work.

To my grandchildren Lily, Emma, Scotty, and Charlie, you are the little loves of my life. You are again reminding me of the importance of being there for the ones we love.

May this book stand as a gentle reminder of the importance of balance, the joy found in shared moments, and the power of love in shaping our lives.

All my love

Endorsements

"Linda has been a constant source of information and encouragement during my due diligence of MRI Network. She is not only professional but cares deeply and that can be seen during our countless conversations. She showcases positivity and played a big part in my choosing of MRI. Her talent and knowledge is above par. Any organization truly can benefit from her skill set and I'm lucky that our paths crossed."

~ Joselin Sams

"Linda helped me with the discovery process, which led to my purchase of an Abrakadoodle franchise, outstanding consultant."

~ Cecilia Nsiah

"Simply put, Linda is really good at her job. She is thoughtful, calm, perceptive, and listens. For someone like me, who has no experience in the complex business of franchising, she makes you feel capable, smart, and guided. I would recommend working with Linda to anyone who is looking for a coach who feels like a friend. She has your best interests in mind."

~ T. Khrestin

"Linda is fantastic to work with and I highly recommend working with her if you're interested in exploring franchising. She's super responsive, took the time to understand my needs, and provided great options that fit my requirements. She also provided great guidance and demonstrated that she had my best interests in mind throughout the process."

~ *W. Rothbauer*

"Working with Linda was a great pleasure. She is very professional, but more importantly, from the first moment we connected, I felt I had a friend for life. She provided exceptional guidance throughout the entire franchise search and acquisition process. Linda was always available and provided expert advice and recommendations. She has high integrity and always looked out for my best interest. I highly recommend Linda for those who are looking for new business opportunities."

~ *T. Scillieri*

"Linda is an amazing guide to the franchising world. She understands both sides of the equation, having owned franchises herself. Her knowledge and experience were invaluable when I embarked on purchasing multiple franchises. I cannot recommend her enough!"

~ *D. Madeira*

"The process of finding a business to purchase can be daunting. Having a professional who gets to know you and works proactively to find the best fit is a rare find indeed. So happy that we had Linda to be a partner, advocate, and advisor. Throughout the process, Linda helped guide us to the ideal acquisition. In addition to the benefit she provided, she displayed tremendous integrity throughout the process and well after the deal was done. She is a rare find in the industry; be sure to connect with her if you are in need of an A+ Franchise Advisor."

~ J. Lombardo

"Linda is an extremely professional and personable advisor. She is patient with you yet motivated for you to succeed. Her knowledge of the franchise world and expertise in guiding you through the process is irreplaceable. Her reputation in the industry is highly respected from every contact that I encounter. I would highly recommend Linda if you are looking to buy a franchise."

~ R. Shoemaker

Foreword

Over twenty-five years ago, I met a very smart young woman who was about to make an important decision. This decision would greatly influence her life, spark many shared memories, and secure our life-long friendship.

Linda Schaeffer and I met when she was looking to step away from a career in accounting to do something that would offer her more flexibility and work-life balance. She found that a home-based franchise where I worked called Computertots offered her that solution. We were both new to the world of franchising and eager to learn. We both recognized early on that franchising was a good fit for our desired lifestyles.

It took courage for Linda to take that first step into franchise ownership. While today, a greater number of women consider business ownership, fewer made that decision in the 1990s. And considering that there were much fewer home-based franchise models to choose from, Linda was very much a pioneer.

In later years, I co-founded Abrakadoodle, an arts education franchise that brings art programs to children worldwide. Linda had sold her Computertots franchise years earlier and became an Abrakadoodle franchise owner. Here we were, together again!

It has been my privilege to witness her being recognized for her achievements with multiple growth and leadership awards. She brings a wealth of experience to the work that she does today as a franchise consultant. Linda pulls from personal experience to help guide those who are considering business ownership. She knows what it is like to consider that important next step and understands how franchise organizations with solid support and training systems can enable success.

Rosemarie Hartnett
President - Abrakadoodle
ICFE Board of Governors, IFA

Table of Contents

PART I -

THE REFLECTION

"The purpose of life is to live it, to taste experience to the utmost, to reach out eagerly and without fear for new and richer experience." ~ Eleanor Roosevelt

———————～——————

As Eleanor Roosevelt so eloquently says, we are not put here on earth to just sit back and let life happen to us. We must reach out, take risks, and step outside of our comfort zone so that we may experience life.

Why is it that so many women find themselves in a time of transition or seeking to achieve a goal without direction or support? From one woman to another, it is time to invest in yourself and pursue your dreams!

For me, change comes easy, and in fact, I think I make people uncomfortable with my need for change. Maybe it stems from moving around a lot as a child. I had to leap in and build a life because it might only be a year or so until we moved again. I became very adaptable, and because of that, I have always loved a challenge and have been comfortable taking risks and trying new things. Transitions in life affect us all, but it's how we handle transitions that make us resilient. Also, being comfortable in who I am, I feel I was very fortunate to have defined my path fairly early in life.

My journey into franchising began back in 1990. I was pregnant with my second child, and I didn't want to endure another tax season as a public accountant. My husband brought home a magazine article that was left on his train seat titled something like "The Top 10 Franchises for Women." In that article was a brand called Computertots, which became my first franchise business. This business would allow me to work from home, which was not common in the '90s. I could have a business, earn a respectable income, yet be home for my children. It was the work-life balance I craved, which was unattainable in the tax accounting world.

In recent years, the business world has witnessed a significant transformation, with an increasing number of women stepping into entrepreneurship, business ownership, and leadership. This shift has been fueled by a multitude of factors, from societal changes to economic opportunities and personal motivations. The '90s were certainly not my parents' generation, but most of my friends in the neighborhood were either stay-at-home moms or worked outside-the-home traditional jobs. Very few, if any, were business owners.

Nevertheless, I took a leap of faith and pursued franchise ownership. Now, after three decades of working in the industry, I have the privilege of helping other women pursue their dreams of business ownership.

I understand that change is not easy for most women. Women were not generally encouraged to take risks. My goal is to share that no matter what stage of life you are in, what career path you've chosen, or the life transition you face, there are options out there for you to achieve your life goals. Could franchise ownership be a fit for you in your next chapter of life? Maybe…maybe not. But either way, this book will introduce you to an option you may never have thought of. At the very least, you will become educated in an industry that has been around for ages—a way to go into business ownership *for* yourself but not *by* yourself.

Ultimately, if you want to pursue franchising as a business opportunity or, better yet, invest in yourself through franchising, I invite you to reach out to me for a consultation call. As my young niece Katie, who left us too early, liked to say, "Live the life you love." I want to inspire each of you reading this to use this opportunity as a launchpad to create a life you love…and hopefully earn a nice living along the way!

Chapter 1:
We've Come A Long Way, Baby!

———————⁓———————

B efore we dive in, I want to share some insights about women in business. Women have had to fight for the right to work outside the home for decades. And surprisingly (or maybe not surprising), in 1965, only 39% of women were in the work force.[1] Today, the workforce is roughly equally divided among men and women. But that is not to say that women are viewed as equals or given the same opportunities. I am not here to debate these facts or the history of women in the workforce. Rather, I share this information to provide a perspective on the opportunities that lay at your feet if you are willing to grab them.

Let's look at some important factors contributing to women's opportunities to step into the roles of entrepreneurs, business, and franchise owners.

A Wealth of Opportunities

One of the primary motivators for women to become entrepreneurs is the pursuit of financial independence. Whatever your reason for considering business ownership, owning and operating a business provides women with the autonomy to contribute to their household income and secure their financial future. I will show you how franchising can create this opportunity.

Despite significant progress over the years across many industries, the gender pay gap persists. I don't want to be on my soapbox, but the reality is that women typically earn less than men. Entrepreneurship allows women to create their own income streams, potentially mitigating the impact of this wage disparity. By setting their own salary standards, women business owners can challenge existing societal norms, create a more equitable business environment, and forge a path for future generations.

Entrepreneurship provides women with the flexibility to balance work and personal life. Many women, especially those with family responsibilities, find the ability to set their own schedules and work from home appealing. This was the main driver for me back in the '90s. Business ownership was the only way I could create the flexible schedule I wanted so badly.

Maybe you have retired from your lifelong career and are looking for your next chapter. You are pursuing opportunities that have flexibility so that you may pursue many new opportunities for this new life stage.

Women entrepreneurs often create businesses that prioritize a supportive and inclusive work environment. This approach is not only beneficial for the women leading these ventures but also fosters a culture of diversity and inclusivity that can positively impact employees and the broader community.

Many female entrepreneurs are driven by a sense of purpose, often aligning their passions and interests with an unmet need in the market or industry. This motivation not only fuels their commitment to their businesses but also contributes to the overall enrichment of diverse industries.

Entrepreneurship offers a pathway for women to break through traditional gender barriers that may exist in corporate environments. By establishing their own businesses, women can create leadership opportunities for themselves and challenge preconceived notions about gender roles in the business world across diverse industries. Along those lines, women also have the opportunity to build supportive networks, both within and outside their industries, and as we will discuss, networking is a critical factor to success in business ownership.

With the evolution of the digital age, women can leverage online platforms, educational resources, and networking opportunities to acquire the skills and knowledge necessary for business success, creating fertile ground for women from diverse backgrounds to venture into entrepreneurship.

Lastly, as society recognizes the importance of fostering gender diversity in entrepreneurship, greater opportunities, such as grants, loans, and incentives for women-owned businesses, become available for more women to enter the entrepreneurial world and to succeed and thrive.

The increasing presence of women in entrepreneurship and business ownership is a testament to the evolving dynamics of the global business landscape. As more women embrace the challenges and opportunities of entrepreneurship, and for this conversation, franchising, they contribute not only to their financial empowerment but also to the overall diversification and success of the business world. Society must continue fostering an environment that supports and encourages women in business, ensuring that the entrepreneurial landscape becomes increasingly inclusive and reflects the diverse talents and perspectives that women bring to the table.

Now that you understand how opportunities for women in business exist, I ask you, "What are you looking to achieve? What has been stopping you from stepping into the world of business ownership? Have you ever considered franchising as an option to help you achieve your goals?"

Within the next chapters, I will ask you to approach these questions honestly and transparently. It's possible by learning about the opportunities that franchising provides, you will be able to determine if franchising could be a good fit for you.

Let's get to work!

Key Takeaways:

Entrepreneurship and business ownership offer women a wealth of opportunities, including:

- New income streams
- Financial independence
- Work-life balance
- New opportunities
- Renewed sense of purpose
- Diversity and inclusion
- Breaking gender barriers
- And many more....

What is your WHY for exploring franchising as an opportunity? Maybe some of the above are part of your WHY— write down some other reasons.

_____

_____

_____

_____

_____

_____

_____

_____

Chapter 2:

How Did You Get Here?

"Women, they have minds, and they have souls, as well as just hearts. And they've got ambition, and they've got talent, as well as just beauty." ~ Louisa May Alcott - Little Women

As a woman, I, too, have all of those amazing characteristics Louisa May Alcott described in Little Women, just as do you. I have a mind, soul, and heart, and as you will see throughout this book, I strive to use all of them earnestly in everything I do.

I have certainly been blessed with gifts and no one has ever accused me of not being ambitious!

I have already shared with you why I am here, why I have written this book, and what I hope you, as the reader, will get out of it. My question for you is, why are you here?

Why did you buy this book?

Something about this book caught your eye. Was it the catchy title? Or the empowering message? Maybe it was my story?

While I hope it was the combination of all the above, more importantly, I hope the reason you bought this book is that you are ready to invest in yourself and live the life you dream about!

The Transitions of Life

So, let's look at some of the things you may be experiencing or where you find yourself at this stage of your life.

- Maybe you are a divorcee and, having received a divorce settlement, are eager to start a business.

- Maybe you have decided to take your parents up on the offer of going to college or money to invest in a business.

- Maybe you have recently started your family and want the flexibility of staying at home but the benefits of working. (This was me as a new mom!)

- Maybe you are giving yourself a birthday present at the age of fifty of investing in yourself through a business opportunity. (I'll tell you this story later....)

- Maybe you have been a stay-at-home mom for years, and now, as an empty nester, you are ready to reenter the workforce, but your skills have not kept up with the times.

- Maybe you are tired of the hustle and bustle of corporate life and are looking for a career change!

- Maybe you are at retirement age and looking to transition into something new and exciting.

- Maybe you and your partner want to do something together, and a business opportunity will give you that togetherness you are looking for.

Do you see a recurring theme here? Maybe a pattern revolving around transition? Of course, you don't need a tragic event or life-changing circumstances to decide to take advantage of a business opportunity. The point is that people often decide to explore franchising when they are in a stage of transition.

The story I referred to above about a woman investing in herself for her birthday occurred in 2015. This woman was one of my first clients and she happened to find me on Google. Because of this, she was local to my area, which made this even more rewarding. I will never forget the first phone call, which went something like this:

> *Hello, this is Linda Schaeffer. Hi, my name is Cara _____. I'm reaching out because, for my 50th birthday, I want to invest in a business for myself. I laughed and said, "That's so funny. I'm turning 50 too but most of my friends are buying themselves plastic surgery, not a franchise!"*

I am sharing this quote not just to make you laugh, although we did both laugh together about it. I share it because a transition can be any change you are experiencing. Her transition was about wanting to give back in this new stage of her life. Her 50's!

We were able to find her a new business that allowed her to continue practicing medicine but also build a community based franchise that would serve seniors and their families.

Let me give you another example of what encouraged the start of one business venture.

The women who started the Computertots franchise were educators. In 1982, on leave from their jobs, they met at a playgroup their children were enrolled in. The children would play and the mothers would talk about children, jobs, etc. Together, Mary and Karen created a business called Educational Computer Workshop, which used computers to tutor children with learning disabilities. They were able to work hours around their own children's schedules, creating a win-win situation. This business then led to them creating Computertots, the first franchise I invested in.

Men certainly have their own reasons for choosing franchise ownership, but that is not why we are here. Many of the reasons I mentioned above may also apply to male candidates and why they read this book, but that is not, in fact, the focus of this book.

Where Are YOU Going?

I am here specifically to show women how investing in themselves can be the difference between where they were and where they see themselves going. Now, of course, there are a multitude of other books about franchising, business opportunities, and possibly thousands on self-improvement.

And while I am not discounting their value or benefit, I can assure you that this book will be very different from any of them.

Why?

Because I completely understand, have lived through, or have coached someone who has experienced many of the same pain points that you have.

As we talked about in the last chapter, women have not always had it easy in the world of business or work, for that matter. I was driven to become a franchise owner as I pursued opportunities that would afford me the flexibility of earning money and raising my family. Thirty years later, I would not change my decision to not only own several franchises but now guide others to do the same.

The times may be different, but many of the pain points around women and business are the same. Franchising, unlike many other business opportunities, seems to be a little-known secret that I believe I am uniquely qualified to share with women because I have been in their shoes. Now, whether your life situation fits into one of those I mentioned above or if you are interested in this opportunity for a completely different reason, it does not matter. What matters is how you envision your life and how I can help you to achieve that goal.

Let's look at some key facts surrounding women in the franchising industry.

First of all, women in business have made significant strides in recent years, contributing to the growth and diversity of the franchising industry. According to the U.S. Senate Committee on Small Business & Entrepreneurship in July 2023, "Of the 33.2 million small businesses in the United States, nearly 13 million of them are women-owned."[2]

In other words, nearly 40% of all small businesses are owned by women! Generating nearly $1.8 trillion per year in revenue, women-owned businesses are leading the charge in the United States' economic development and prosperity. This report continues on to say that "Women's economic empowerment is central to women's rights and gender equality. Their access to economic opportunity is essential to a nation's economic prosperity and productivity. In the U.S. economy alone, if female labor market participation grew to the levels seen in other developed economies, the economy could receive a $1 trillion boost over the next 10 years."

Since we also looked back at the numbers of women in the workforce in 1965, it is important to also look at the number of women-owned businesses around the same time. In 1972, when the U.S. Census Bureau first began tracking female entrepreneurship, it was estimated there were only 400,000 businesses owned by women. What an astounding contrast the business world has seen in the last fifty years.

The question is, how do you think this unimaginable increase of more than 3000% happened? One woman, one business, one franchise at a time! It takes all of us collectively to do our part in contributing to this impact.

Let's look at several other facts about franchising, in particular, that contribute to those amazing figures.

- The number of women involved in franchising has been on the rise, with an increasing number of women-owned franchises and female franchisees.

- Women are present across a wide range of industries within franchising, including food and beverage, retail, healthcare, and more.

- Franchising provides women with entrepreneurial opportunities without the need to start a business from scratch. The established business model and support from the franchisor can be particularly appealing to women looking to enter the business world.

- There has been a growing recognition of the need for support networks for women in franchising. Organizations, conferences, and networking events specifically cater to women, providing them with resources, mentorship, and connections.

- Some franchisors actively promote diversity and encourage women to become franchisees. They may offer financial incentives, training programs, and ongoing support to women interested in this particular type of business opportunity.

Why Choose Me?

If you have not figured it out yet, I am passionate about franchising. I have worked with dozens of clients, teaching them about franchising as a business ownership option, guiding them through the process, and watching them create the lives they wanted. Now, not everyone I have worked with has chosen to go this route, and we will talk about this more later. In fact, the whole point of working with me is to better understand what franchising is and its benefits and find the franchise brand that is best suited for you.

Ultimately, this business is an investment in yourself, and so it must be a good fit.

My experiences have been no different.

Let me jump back and tell you about all three of my franchise experiences. My first franchise was Computertots, as I mentioned before. After my husband found that magazine on the train, I scheduled my visit to the home office to meet the team. I found myself so impressed by Mary Rogers and Karen Marshall and their passions for the program that I left agreements in hand. Introducing preschoolers to computers at a time when parents were afraid of computers themselves was a joy! My role was to market the program to YMCAs, Recreation Centers, and Preschools. Daycare directors were thrilled to have us come in as an enrichment program. It gave them an edge against other daycares who didn't offer such a program. At the peak of our time with Computertots, we were the "Top Producer" in the franchise system, reaching over 1200 students each week. This was a time I will never forget. It taught me I could do anything I put my mind to and that taking risks can bring great rewards. I sold my last territory of Computertots in 1997, just before my 3rd child was born, to one of my teachers, Deb Evans, who would go on to do great things in franchising.

After my son Matt was school age, I got the bug again to own a business. Luckily for me, I found that Mary Rogers had teamed with another Computertots colleague and formed Abrakadoodle. This time, it was Art Enrichment instead of Computers. Mary and Rosemarie found that with all of the budget cuts in the arts, there was a need for art enrichment. Not every child wants to play sports. Some little ones want to create! So what did I do? I hopped back on Amtrak and made my way back to Virginia to the Abrakadoodle headquarters and became franchise #6. I bought the entire Philadelphia and South Jersey area and jumped right back in where I left off. This time, marketing was easier because I had established such great connections in the educational enrichment market that directors welcomed me and my new program back because they knew I would take good care of their parents and children. Abrakadoodle was an immense success working with children as young as 18 months old up through grade school.

After five years of owning and operating Abrakadoodle, I once again decided to sell my business and again, I sold to one of my teachers. It was a mother-and-daughter team who continued to run the business for over 15 years. Another successful and very rewarding journey in franchising for me. In fact, one of my teachers later opened their own daycare franchise, where my grandchildren attended and were taken very good care of!!!!

So, what would my life look like without franchise ownership? Well, this is where I went on to work with Abrakadoodle as a development person, helping them bring in great new franchisees. I certainly knew the "day in the life" of an Abrakadoodle owner, so who better to interview and work with prospective franchisees? I not only worked in development with Abrakadoodle, but I also helped Crestcom and MRI Network. Each of these roles helped me understand the various ways franchisors recruit and train new franchisees.

In 2015 I began my career that has led me to this book. I now felt like I had what it takes to work as a franchise advisor. I now felt the confidence that prospective franchisees would choose me to work with because I had seen and worked on all sides of franchising and, most importantly, had been in their shoes, not once but twice, and later will be a third time. I'll talk about that later on in the book.

I made the leap three times and never once regretted my decision. Having experience in franchise ownership, management, and sales, as well as being a CPA, I have a unique perspective when assisting those looking into franchise ownership. I have walked your walk and know how scary the idea of business ownership can be. I excel in building and maintaining strong personal relationships with those who are serious about investigating real opportunities.

I am a published author and have been featured in Adoption Today, Franchise Connect, The Philadelphia Inquirer, First for Women magazine, and Franchise Times Guide to Selecting, Buying and Owning a Franchise.

Let me share with you what one person has written about me and the services I offer:

> *"Working with Linda was a great pleasure. She is very professional, but more importantly, from the first moment we connected, I felt I had a friend for life. She provided exceptional guidance throughout the entire franchise search and acquisition process. Linda was always available and provided expert advice and recommendations. She has high integrity and always looked out for my best interest. I highly recommend Linda for those who are looking for new business opportunities ." ~ Toni*

You may be thinking that I am sharing all of this and even writing this book, in fact, to convince you to buy something from me. In fact, that idea of selling something to you could not be farther from the truth. It all boils down to my providing a unique service that is well worth the time—at no cost!

As a Broker/Consultant, I earn my living by connecting qualified franchisees with brands. It is in my (and their) best interest to ensure a good fit so that, ultimately, everyone comes out a winner. In reality, there's no financial reason for someone *not* to work with me because the franchisor is not allowed to charge them a lesser franchise fee because they didn't have a broker.

Consider me a matchmaker of sorts, matching your interests, financial resources, and reasons for considering franchising as a business option, with companies interested in expanding their territory, exposure, and brand recognition.

Not convinced? Consider that I have closed a large number of deals. More importantly, I have helped dozens of people achieve their goals through franchising.

Franchising Is Personal

Franchising is very personal. Not only is it near and dear to my heart, but I understand the very personal motivations why someone may consider business ownership. Therefore, I need to deeply understand each client's motivations and goals before I can make recommendations for the best fit. In the next chapters, we will walk through the process of determining your why, what drives you, and where you want franchising to take you.

But it is a very viable option for many women, one that is underestimated and underexplored. It is my goal to enlighten you about its many benefits and then help you find the brand that best fits you and your needs.

However, I also want to caution you that just because you may have money to invest in a business, it does not necessarily mean that franchising is right for you. Conversely, just because you may not think you have enough money to invest, it doesn't mean that you should abandon business ownership. The goal in working with me is for us to explore all of your options and evaluate why, or in some cases, why not, owning a franchise may be valuable to you. Not your sister, daughter, or friend, but to you! I told you it was personal, right?

So, at this point, I hope I have shared enough about myself, what I do, and franchising as a business option that you will consider reaching out to me for a consultation call. If you choose not to read this book any further and/or determine that franchising is not for you, I wish you all the best and no hard feelings.

I would be remiss, though, if I did not pose this one last question before you go: what would prevent you from moving forward and at least exploring this option?

As I mentioned, there is no harm or risk in working with me, and it does not cost you anything. I guarantee that even if you simply are more educated about a business opportunity, you will walk away having received a big value.

If you are eager to live the life you love, why not give it a shot?

Key Takeaways:

Consider this: what transition brought you here? Where are you going and what drives you?

Ultimately, I am a matchmaker and it is my goal to pair you with the franchise opportunity that best suits you.

Use this space to do a brain dump and envision where you see yourself in 5, 10, or even 20 years. Be bold and dare to dream!

_____

_____

_____

_____

_____

_____

_____

_____

Chapter 3:

Be Who You Are

"Knowing yourself is the beginning of all wisdom." ~
Aristotle

T o re-quote Aristotle, "Knowing yourself is the beginning of all wisdom." I truly believe this to be true and will even take this one step further. As Lao Tzu, a legendary Chinese philosopher, said, "Knowing others is intelligence; knowing yourself is true wisdom. Mastering others is strength; mastering yourself is true power."

How many people do you know have tapped into the power that we all possess inside of ourselves? Of course, I don't want to get all philosophical on you, but let's just think about this for a minute. I know countless women (in particular) who have been "searching" to find their purpose for most of their lives. We are often defined by what we "do" versus who we "are," causing many of us to wander through life, never truly walking in purpose for no other reason than we have not yet discovered who we *are*.

For example, I remember when my children were in school, identifying myself as "Sam's mom" or even "Scott's wife" at social gatherings. If I wasn't comfortable with who I am as "Linda," I could have very easily been persuaded to believe that those roles defined me. But as I mentioned earlier, I knew my path, so I was able to use my power of knowing myself as my wisdom to succeed in my career. Don't get me wrong, when my son scored the winning goal in hockey, or my daughter won a match with her killer serve, or my youngest won the 400IM, I happily screamed out I'm "Kevin's, Samantha's, or Matt's mom!"

On a serious note, I know so many of my friends who, despite being well-educated, career women, struggled to identify with who they are at the core. They were labeled as "CEO," "that horrible boss," "so and so's mom," or "Susan's daughter." But who are they really? And the bigger question is, are they happy being pigeonholed into a role? While I am very happy being Me'Me' to my grandchildren, mom to my children, Scott's wife, and *the* franchise advisor, I also know that my true happiness comes from knowing myself more deeply. In fact, this is where my true calling steps in, allowing me to be comfortable in who I am and help others to find their true power.

So, why do I say all of this? I don't want to take you down the road of this being a touchy-feely self-help book, but I do think that the key to success in business and life is knowing who you are and, almost as important, who you are *not*!

Dr. Tasha Eurich is an organizational psychologist, researcher, and author who says it like this in her book "Insight: The Surprising Truth About How Others See Us, How We See Ourselves, and Why the Answers Matter More Than We Think."

"There is strong scientific evidence that people who know themselves and how others see them are happier. They make smarter decisions. They have better personal and professional relationships. They raise more mature children. They're smarter, superior students who choose better careers. They're more creative, more confident, and better communicators."

Now, doesn't that sound like someone we should all be? If everyone on the planet were to take the time to really discover who they are, the world would be a much better place. I am certain of it. But since we cannot impose this thought or even the desire on everyone, we have to settle for doing our part to discover our own wisdom and unlock our true power.

You are probably scratching your head right now, wondering what in the world this has to do with franchising. Well, in fact, everything! As we will see in the next chapters, part of what I do to help clients achieve the life they want to live is determine a fit by using questionnaires, tools, and lots of conversation.

Imagine this: you come to me looking to make tons of money, travel, live a luxurious lifestyle, and drive a fancy car. Ok, so maybe you were a high-powered executive somewhere, and now this is something you want to do in "retirement." While these are amazing things to desire and accomplishments to achieve, do you have what it takes to own a business, become an entrepreneur, and do it on your own? What is the "why" behind your motivations and desires? How will achieving these goals make you feel?

I am not a licensed therapist or counselor, nor do I profess to be able to change your life with therapy, coaching, or medication. No—I am an advisor who sincerely believes that finding the right "fit" is more than half the battle, and by *not* doing the work to identify who you are at your core, you (and I) will be laying the foundation for failure.

Now, I don't believe anything or anyone is ever a failure but rather something that we learn. However, when it comes to starting a business, which inherently comes with its own risks, I'd rather approach the situation with wisdom and understanding than from a place of discomfort, fear, and anxiety. Of course, just because you may have a firm grasp of who you are doesn't change the fact that stepping into entrepreneurship can be scary, anxiety-inducing, and risky. The goal is to find the brand that best suits you based on who you are, your interests, passions, skills, and goals.

I encourage you to consider this statement for a minute: who are you? In my role as a franchise advisor, I would be remiss if I didn't take the time to really get to know you. But there is no point in us proceeding any further if you are unwilling to take a good look at yourself to understand what you want out of life, what you don't want, and how you see your life and dreams.

When I think of my niece Katie, who lost her life at a young age, I am reminded of the mantra she lived by: "Live the life you love and Love the life you live." As her disease progressed and she was undergoing treatment, she would talk about how upsetting it was to her that people weren't making the most of the life they were given. She had so many dreams she would never be able to see come true, it made her angry when people wasted their own chances at happiness. Now, there is no shame in the game—many people walk around with a mask, hiding their true selves from others or, frankly, denying themselves from acknowledging who they are and walking in their purpose. I firmly believe that we are all capable of being happy, which begins with discovering our true selves and then following our dreams.

Again, this may sound like I am standing on my soapbox, trying to get you to buy a self-help course or follow my journey (both of which are good), but in reality, my goal is to lay the foundation on which you will take that next step. To reiterate Eleanor Roosevelt's message, "The purpose of life is to live it, to taste experience to the utmost, to reach out eagerly and without fear for new and richer experiences."

So, I say all of that to talk about several invaluable keys to success in life and business, all of which begin with knowing who you are and, possibly even more importantly, knowing who you are not.

Be Who You REALLY Are

Of course, we've all been told since we were children to follow our dreams, be ourselves, and don't let anything stop us. But then life happens and many of us find ourselves on a path or journey that we never expected or wished for. Many people lose sight of themselves, but I urge you to be comfortable with who you really are, get back to those things that you love, and discover your relationship with yourself. This will guide you toward leading the life you want.

In Part II, we will dive into the discovery process and identify characteristics that define you, your goals, and your wishes.

Know Who You Are NOT

I've said it before, but knowing who you are **not** may be even more important than knowing who you are. However, having the wisdom to know the traits, skills, and characteristics that you don't have is a powerful tool in understanding and setting direction.

Let me give you an example. My friend, Susan, was in the corporate world for many years. While she could deliver a well-organized, impactful presentation to a room full of co-workers, she was, in fact, terrified each and every time she had to stand up at the front of the room. Could she be a speaker or presenter for a living? Could she start a business in which she had to speak in front of hundreds or thousands of people? Knowing herself as she does, Susan knows that although she is capable of doing this, she is not a speaker at heart, preferring to work behind the scenes, navigating the inner workings of a business, and working one-on-one with individuals rather than in front of a group. I worked with Susan to identify brands where she could be hands-on, interacting directly with customers and clients, making an impact in a business that fit her. How did I know what type of franchise would be best for Susan? She knew what she was not.

Be Comfortable with Rejection

We all experience rejection every day in everything that we do. Don't believe me?

- Your joke didn't make anyone laugh

- The new coworker at the office introduces herself to everyone except you

- Your friends forgot to leave a seat for you at the restaurant where you are meeting them for lunch

So, while these may not seem to be outright rejections, nevertheless, they can stir those feelings of rejection in us, whether we identify them as such or not. The thing is, rejection of any kind is uncomfortable, and people internalize rejection differently. But rejection is part of life.

On the other hand, rejection and the feelings it stirs up do not define you. In fact, accepting that rejection is normal allows you to learn and grow from every experience.

Fear Factor

Have you ever met someone who has big dreams and aspirations but has never taken any action toward achieving what they want? Maybe you have not taken that leap to leave your job or start a business. Fear can be debilitating and one of the primary reasons people do not live the life they want. Imagine what your life may be like if you had taken the chance.

Of course, fear is a normal reaction to all life throws at us, and while it is very cliché, it is how we handle it that makes the difference between happiness and, well, anything else. There is so much to be afraid of in life:

- Fear of losing money
- Fear of rejection
- Fear of loss or failure
- Fear of making a mistake
- Fear of disappointment (self and others)
- Fear of judgment
- Fear of change
- Fear of the unknown
- Fear of success

Of all the fears I have listed, the last one is the most baffling. I know quite a few people, men and women, who have made the conscious decision not to pursue what they want in life in fear of actually succeeding. If they did, they might actually destroy all of the beliefs they have thought and been told about themselves.

Is that you? Are you afraid that if you step out and take a risk, and if there is the possibility that you are successful, something will happen? I assure you that the only thing that will happen is happiness itself!

The reality is that fear holds many people back from taking the bull by the horns and living the life they want. My job as a franchise advisor is to help you evaluate the risks, answer the financial questions, and understand the unknowns so that you can make the decision that you will not fear or be disappointed by.

I heard a story of a woman who worked at a 9 to 5 job but was miserable. She knew what her true calling and purpose were and wanted to start a business doing what she loved. But fear…. It wasn't until the pandemic hit and she was let go that she looked fear in the eyes and decided to move forward afraid. Her hand was forced when she was terminated, and rather than look for another full-time position, she took her future into her own hands. Fear had been holding her back, but once she was forced to the edge, she had no choice but to jump. And it has turned out to be a great decision. Had the pandemic not changed her job situation for her, would she have chosen to take the leap, thereby possibly staying in that job, unhappy and unfulfilled?

The question right now is, what is holding you back?

Risk Tolerance

Of course, there are always factors that can derail your plans at every step of the way. Business and life in general are risky. For example, the COVID-19 pandemic presented the franchise industry with many challenges as candidates could not evaluate businesses and the world was under strict lockdown restrictions, preventing movement.

Now, remember I mentioned earlier that I had purchased a third franchise business? In 2019, I got very excited about a boutique fitness brand catering to the over-50 crowd. This brand has unique equipment that helps folks build strength in a safe and effective manner. I thought this would be an amazing business for me to own semi-absentee and one that my youngest son, Matt, a college swimmer and fitness buff, would want to work in.

I got really excited about their proprietary equipment and the target audience of the brand which was me!

(Note to self: first red flag not to buy a brand is because you want to use their service!)

I purchased four territories, thinking it would be a great business to own and a terrific job for Matt, who had his own big dreams.

(Another note to self: make sure the person you're investing in wants to be invested in.)

Well, guess what happened? I had my grand opening on February 1, 2020. I spent my grand opening marketing budget and, just 6 weeks later, had to close because of the pandemic. Reopening in New Jersey, of all states, was brutal, and getting the over-50 crowd to feel comfortable coming back to a fitness studio was not an easy task, with multiple challenges and roadblocks. I just wasn't up for the challenge and my son never said he had any interest in the business (that was all just me).

Since Matt had moved on to his dreams of a military career and was about to excel beyond belief, I sold my gym to another owner who was thrilled to take it over. I am happy to say he is thriving today!

This was my third happy ending in franchising but it was certainly a very different story than expected.

The pandemic was an unforeseen and unavoidable interruption to business. However, there are a multitude of other factors that could create a hiccup in the process. From financing issues to contractual changes to timing, life and business can be unpredictable. I say all of this to tell you that, as with any other decision or challenge we face in life, we must learn from our mistakes (as I did with the failed franchise business) and develop alternate plans to keep us on the road to success. So many factors can disrupt even the best of intentions; the idea is to remember that things happen which may be out of your control and which do not reflect on you as failures.

No one ever guaranteed that life or decisions would be easy. And certainly, life has a way of throwing curve balls, but I assure you that I am with you every step of the way as you evaluate the options and make your selection, all the way to Decision Day and beyond.

Money Management

As I mentioned in the last section, people often do not take a leap into a business venture or investment out of fear of losing money. And while there is certainly a risk, there is also a potential for success. Sadly, many people are too focused on the what if…and the negative to consider the what if….and the positive!

Regardless of the type of business or career you are engaged in, money management is an important skill for anyone to have. How do you create a budget or prioritize projects and expenses if you do not have some familiarity with money management? In some high schools, it is now mandatory that all students participate in a basic financial management course. In my opinion, this skill is as critical as any math, science, or history class they are required to take.

How can we send young people out into the world if they do not understand the basics of earning, saving, spending, and investing? Well, if you have been around any young people, you will see that they have the spending down for the most part. But I digress!

Did the mothers of the 1950s have the same decision-making power or financial control we do today? Did they have money at their disposal to start businesses or invest in their future? While some may have been the financial managers of their households, it was more than likely the few rather than the majority. That being said, we live in different times now with greater numbers of women on their own, with their own resources, and willing to become entrepreneurs. Thus, the greater importance of understanding the concepts of money management.

Now, I am not suggesting you have to be a CPA (like me) or have an education in economics. Still, if you are considering taking a risk of any kind, possibly investing in a franchise, you will need to have a good grasp of your own finances as well as how to evaluate a business venture.

In the next section of this book and as part of my process as a franchise advisor, I will walk you through some of the financial risks and what to look for in choosing a brand that fits, looking at the financial expectations, resources required, and any associated fees. I will also introduce you to experts in funding franchises. It's good to know when to let the experts do what they do and stick with what we do and know.

Relationship-building

So, as you may have guessed by now, it is very important to not only know who you are but, more importantly, to *be* who you are. It is no surprise that people want to be around those who are authentic and genuine. I have found in my many years in business that I can spot someone who is trying to be someone they are not from a mile away. How? They seem so uncomfortable in their skin as they strive to be anyone but who they were meant to be.

Why is this important?

If I can spot them, don't you think others will too?

We often get so caught up in life, striving for what we think we want and being who we think others want us to be, that we forget (or have not yet discovered) who we truly are. As I mentioned earlier, knowing who you are leads to wisdom and, ultimately, happiness. But on the larger scale of life, being who you are will attract others who are either like you or want to be around people like you.

David Ogilvy, widely revered as a founding father of modern advertising, is famously quoted as writing, "'If you always hire people who are smaller than you, we shall become a company of dwarfs. If, on the other hand, you always hire people who are bigger than you, we shall become a company of giants." This very profound statement tells me several things:

1. Surround yourself with people you aspire to be like.

2. If you think about yourself in a certain way, possibly small and incapable, you will only attract others like yourself.

If you present to others something you are not, you may only serve to attract others who are doing the same thing. And who wants to be around a bunch of imposters?

Speaking of imposters, the imposter syndrome is a well-documented pattern of behaviors of self-doubt and ineptitude. Therefore, we try to be someone we are not!

If you are familiar with the Steven Spielberg film *Catch Me If You Can*, Leonardo DiCaprio plays the role of a young con artist who has successfully pulled the wool over the world's eyes. While this dramatization is comical on the big screen, in real life, we often do this so subtly that it goes unnoticed by others until it really matters…in relationships.

Of course, being yourself is important in personal and intimate relationships such as with our spouse, friends, family, and significant others, but the importance of it cannot be understated in the world of business.

Although we may be hesitant to admit it, everything revolves around relationships. According to Sam Kaufman of the Forbes Business Council, "Building relationships is possibly the most important skill an entrepreneur can acquire if they're looking to grow a real company. You need to have the ability to acquire, maintain, nurture and grow relationships."[3]

In fact, relationships can be categorized as the most important asset in your business. Think about it: how could you generate revenue without relationships with clients/customers? Who would work with or for you if you cannot build relationships? What about financial institutions and lenders…will anyone simply want to give you money without building connections and relationships? I would never have been able to jump in with Abrakadoodle and reconnect with all of my Computertots clients if we hadn't built strong relationships in the past. Because of the connections we made then, I was able to have a jumpstart into the business.

While I urge you to strive to know yourself and be who you authentically are, I always want to stress the importance of building rapport and making connections. You can still be yourself, even if you are an introvert or quiet and shy. This does not mean that you cannot build and nurture relationships. We will work together to find a brand that allows you to work with warm leads. We will have to find you a brand that you relate to and will allow you to present your brand to people and understand that thing that will make them remember you!

It all boils down to finding the business venture or franchise that best suits who you are, including how you are best at relationship-building. We will take a closer look at how you choose to build relationships in the next chapter as we start to look deeper at your characteristics, preferences, and goals.

Now, at this point, I completely understand if you do not want to read any further. Maybe this part of the book has been too invasive or not what you expected. I assure you that the meat of what we are going to be talking about is just a page away.

This chapter was very important in laying the foundation on which the rest of the book will sit. I needed to prepare you for conversations to follow as we dive deeper into investing in yourself through franchising.

If you elect to put this book down, I respect that and hope I have imparted even just a little bit of wisdom to you. I wish you the best of luck in life and business.

However, if you are going to stick with me, buckle up and get ready for the ride!

Key Takeaways:

To reiterate:

I am not a licensed therapist or counselor, nor do I profess to be able to change your life with therapy, coaching, or medication.

The goal is to find the brand that best suits you based on who you are, your interests, passions, skills, and goals.

Keys to success in life and business:

- Be who you really are
- Know who you are *not*
- Be comfortable with rejection
- Fear factor
- Risk tolerance
- Money management
- Relationship-building

What are your interests? Passions? What makes you unique or what gift do you have to bring to the world? Dig deep and write down all of those things that make you who you are?

_____
_____
_____
_____
_____
_____
_____

What are you afraid of?

_____
_____
_____
_____
_____
_____

How much risk are you willing to take to live the life you desire?

_____
_____
_____
_____
_____
_____

PART II –

THE EXPLORATION

"Investing in yourself is the best investment you will ever make. It will not only improve your life; it will improve the life of all those around you." ~ *Robin Sharma*

In the following chapters, we will dive into the meat of this subject and, more than likely, the reason you purchased this book. I will walk you through the process I use to help you discover who you are, why you are interested in a business venture, and, specifically, why you are interested in a franchise opportunity.

With thirty years of experience in franchising, I will share with you every aspect of the franchise discovery process and walk you through taking this very important and worthwhile step toward financial freedom and living the life you want.

Chapter 4:

What Is a Franchise?

"In business for yourself, but not by yourself." ~ Ray Kroc

———————～——————

In a broad sense, franchising is a business model through which a company creates its expansion strategy. Think about some of the popular businesses near you, such as McDonald's, Dunkin, or Supercuts. Each of these companies has chosen to expand its footprint and, therefore, consumer reach by contracting with franchisees (entrepreneurs and future business owners) to operate the businesses under their logo and brand.

Of course, this is not the only type of business model an organization can use to increase its market share. For example, Starbucks does not franchise, but rather every location worldwide is corporately owned. Because a franchisee is buying into the corporation's business, every franchise location is operated in the same way, just as if the corporation owned it. Like in the examples above, you may not even be able to tell which companies operate as franchises or not. *It should be a business in a box!*

Forbes magazine defines a franchise as: "A method of distributing products or services involving a franchisor, who establishes the brand's trademark or trade name and a business system and a franchisee, who pays a royalty and often an initial fee for the right to do business under the franchisor's name and system."

This is just one of many methods of distributing products and services companies may choose from, depending on their goals, desired outcomes, and market.

As stated, some companies choose to grow their brand before franchising, while others start a company with the specific intent of expanding through franchising. This decision may depend on the industry, competitors, and whether retail or service providers.

Here's an example of each.

XXX Home Care has been open for 20 years and wants to grow their business. They open a second office in another state and it also does well. The franchisor now realizes that they have a "business in a box." This enables them to franchise the concept successfully.

On the other side, we have YYY Nail Salon. The founders of a very successful hair-cutting franchise decided that nails would be a great addition to the offerings of their existing brand. They decided to start a franchise that will offer nail services and franchisees will open next to the existing hair franchises. Whichever reason for choosing franchising as the way to grow the brand, there is a franchise opportunity for everyone who wants it and who is a good fit for the model.

Franchising as an Option

"Optimism is the faith that leads to achievement. Nothing can be done without hope and confidence." ~ Helen Keller

According to a Zapier-commissioned Harris-Poll survey, "Roughly three in five Americans (61 percent) have had an idea for starting a business, and around one third (34 percent) have had more than one. But an overwhelming majority of those people—92 percent—didn't follow through with turning their idea into reality."[4]

Why?

Think about all of the reasons you may have considered starting a business venture and may not have done so at this point:

- Fear (#1 reason which we've talked about)
- Access to funding and financial resources
- Healthcare/benefits
- Lack of information about running a business

Many people and I am not singling out women here, are hesitant about starting a business for a variety of reasons and possibly more than the simple list I provided. As the quote above by Ray Kroc indicates, I want to stress that franchising is a way to go into business ownership *for yourself but not by yourself.* It is a means of going into business and earning a living, yet not having to create a business idea from scratch.

I want to share with you some of the many proven advantages of considering franchising as an option:

1. The franchisor has an established business model, structure, and support system in place for the franchisee to follow and lean on.

2. Name recognition helps keep you top of mind with customers. Being part of a franchise system helps customers feel confident using you vs. an unknown brand.

3. An established network of franchisees provides a level of added support both operationally and emotionally. The sharing of best practices helped franchisees weather the recent pandemic.

4. The collective buying power of a large number of franchisees assists with lowering the costs of supplies, materials, and other essentials.

5. Ongoing training keeps your franchise system at the top of its game!

6. According to 2019 research based on census data, the 2-year franchise success rate is 8% higher than the independent business success rate.

Of course, these benefits just scratch the surface of the many wonderful things that you can and will experience from becoming a business owner of any kind. On a personal level, imagine the joy and pride of knowing you are an entrepreneur. What about the other people's lives you are impacting? Customers who may not have been exposed to this product or service. Employees who get to earn a salary and provide for their families. Never mind your own family and personal finances, who can reap the rewards of your hard work.

I want to point out that there are also many intangible rewards that I have discovered through franchising.

- My children get to see me not only as a wage earner and contributor to the household but as a successful entrepreneur making a difference.
- I was making an impact in the community, helping other families and the local economy.

I worked with a young mother who wanted to be a business owner for the flexibility of managing her own schedule. She was a recent divorcee with two elementary-age girls. As we worked together and identified the best brand to meet her needs, she discovered something even greater than earning a nice living to support her family. She was setting an example for her daughters as they watched with wide-eyed amazement as their mother struck out on this journey, creating the life for them that they were all proud of and setting an example for them to aspire to. When she came to me to purchase a second brand, she was elated to have started down this road and was looking forward to what the future held not only for her but for her daughters. She felt as if she had just changed the trajectory of future generations with her decision and could not have been more proud.

Funny enough, that is how I felt about my experience with franchising. When I was in my 30s owning Computertots, my children, 2 and 6, were surrounded by computers and software; they were my guinea pigs. One day, my husband came home from his very stressful, high-paying corporate job. He was tired and my young son asked him why he was tired, continuing, "Mommy should be tired because she is the boss of her business." I chuckled but absolutely loved it!

So, I draw your attention back to my initial comments in Part I about the various types of transitions. During our initial consultation, I will ask you why you are interested in a business venture. What is the transition that is prompting you to consider going down this road NOW?

Although franchising is certainly a viable business option and I have shown how it has many benefits, is it right for everyone? Of course not. I would ask you about any decision or option in your life. Is going to college for you? Which state is the best location for you? Is an electric car the right purchase for you? Should you buy or rent a home?

There are so many factors that go into making a decision that is right **for you**, and in fact, the decision to embark on any business journey should not be taken lightly. But I assure you that I will be here for you every step of the way to find the franchise brand that is right for you.

Back to the question, who is franchising for? Well, the easy answer is that it is for everyone, but I would be stretching it a bit. In fact, franchising is *not* a good fit for everyone and if we work together, I will be honest enough to tell you that as well.

I will use various tools to answer this question—is franchising right for you? In the next chapter, we will take a deep dive into your characteristics, traits, and preferences to help me determine the best fit for you.

Can You Be a Franchisee?

So, I just asked a very big and powerful question—is franchising right for you?

I cannot reiterate enough that it is completely okay if we deem that franchising as a business or investment opportunity is just not the right fit for you. Now that you have learned all about what franchising is and hopefully learned a little bit more about yourself, it is fine if you decide if it is simply not right for you. Remember, I am here at your service simply to help you, not sell you anything.

The point is that just because traditional franchising may not be right (or right now), it does not mean that you cannot become an entrepreneur or a business owner. There are a variety of alternative business options that I encourage you to explore, including:

- Biz Opp - Business opportunities don't necessarily follow a standardized model. There are usually no ongoing fees like royalties. There is an initial fee to learn the business and have rights to certain systems and processes, but most times, there is not an ongoing relationship. One of the first brands I helped a candidate invest in was a social media marketing brand. It was not a franchise but a Biz-Opp. He signed an agreement and paid an initial fee, but then he was pretty much on his own to operate any way he chose.

- Licensee - Being a licensee of a business means that you have purchased the rights to use certain aspects of the business's intellectual property, brand, or proprietary information and may operate that business under the licensing agreement. Being a licensee often means adopting and following a specific business model established by the licensor. This can include adhering to operational procedures, marketing strategies, and other guidelines set by the business owner. Licensees make money by capitalizing on the brand they have licensed with.

- Distributorship - In simple terms, a distributorship is a business arrangement where one company (the distributor) is given the right to sell and distribute products or services of another company (the supplier) within a specific area or market. The distributor buys the products from the supplier at a wholesale price and then sells them to retailers, other distributors, or directly to customers, typically earning a profit through markups. The agreement between the distributor and the supplier outlines the terms and conditions of their partnership, including the geographic area where the distributor has the exclusive right to sell the products. When I think of a distributorship, I think of many of the retail brands like Coca-Cola. They allow establishments to sell their brand and make money off of the markup. Interior designers have that same relationship with many fabric companies.

- Consultant - In a business relationship, think of a consultant as a professional who provides expert advice, guidance, and specialized knowledge to help a company improve its performance, solve problems, or achieve specific goals. Consultants are typically hired on a temporary basis to address particular challenges or provide strategic insights, offering external perspectives and expertise to support the client's business objectives. Many of the candidates I work with are working as consultants to earn extra income while growing their businesses. This allows a lot of flexibility.

- Organic business owner - Of course, one option for all of you is to create your own brand from the bottom up. If you are not comfortable entering into any agreements with anyone, then this may be the best option for you.

- Freelancer - You could choose to be a freelancer, which means you would be self-employed and offer your services to clients on a project-by-project basis rather than being employed by a single company. You would be able to work independently and have flexibility in choosing your own projects. You would not be bound to a long-term contract with any single employer and would get to work with multiple clients simultaneously.

I worked with a wonderful woman, Leyla, back in 2021, who was exploring franchise ownership with me.

Here's her story….

> *I connected with Linda when I was exploring different career paths for myself, including franchise ownership. From the very first call, I was impressed by Linda's clear & honest communication style, pleasant personality, and deep professionalism. She patiently took me through the whole process from education on franchise business to helping me to focus on the ones which met expectations and requirements. All the franchises she brought to my consideration were great. Patiently, she helped me to short-list to one franchise, which I seriously considered proceeding with. The only reason why I didn't proceed was that I decided to go with my personal career coaching business. I didn't purchase the franchise, but Linda and I have established great working relations, which I truly appreciate. I am looking forward to staying connected with Linda as I enjoyed working with her.*

I will go back to Chapter 3, where we thoroughly discussed being who *you* are. Forcing a franchise opportunity simply because it seems like a prosperous endeavor defeats the purpose of your why if it does not fit with who you are. You have to be true to yourself to truly reap the rewards of any business opportunity!

I want to be clear that franchising is just one path in the transition from corporate to business ownership or wherever you are in your transition to living the life you love.

Key Takeaways:

Franchising is a business in a box. It is an opportunity to go into business *for* yourself but not *by* yourself.

Just because traditional franchising may not be right (or right now), it does not mean that you cannot become an entrepreneur or a business owner.

How do you envision your ideal business?

_____

_____

_____

_____

_____

_____

_____

_____

_____

_____

_____

_____

_____

Chapter 5:

Painting the Picture

"Be yourself.... everyone else is already taken." ~ Oscar Wilde

―――――――――∼―――――――

Now that you have decided to continue learning about franchising and whether it could be a good fit for your life goals, it's time to begin my process of determining what franchise brand may be a good fit for you based on your preferences and goals.

This process begins by gathering information from various sources, including questionnaires, surveys, and a consultation call. We want to work together to paint a picture of what the best-fit franchise would look like.

My Toolbox

As I explained in Chapter 3, you have to be who you are, and it is completely ok if you decide that franchising is not for you. But understand that by becoming a franchise owner, you are investing in yourself and your financial future, making it even more important that it is a good fit.

For my toolbox, I will ask for your resume, an online confidential questionnaire, a LinkedIn profile, and possibly even a franchise culture profile. Why do I need all of this information to help find brands to present? It's simple. Because no two of my clients are the same. Each of you has your own story and your own "why." By having all of these tools, I can really be sure that by the end of our consultation call, I know who you are and what you are trying to accomplish.

I previously mentioned something called a franchise culture profile. Let me explain. Years ago, I met Rebecca Monet at a franchise consultant conference. She was exhibiting her Zorakle profile tool, the Zorakle SpotOn! Profile, which was created specifically for the franchise world. Rebecca created her profile to help the franchise world match candidates to the best-fit franchise for them. Although personality tests have been used by employers for many years, the SpotOn! Profile is not a personality test. It does not just assign personality attributes or traits. People change and therefore, a profile needs to reflect more than just static attributes. As a behavioral scientist, Rebecca studied all of this before creating her unique profile. The Zorakle SpotOn! profile was created to help franchise consultants and franchisors match potential franchisees to brands where they will best fit into their franchise culture, validate well, use the systems and processes provided, and have the competencies to grow a successful business. The SpotOn! profile looks at cultures, values, competencies, leadership skills, and stages of growth **of both the franchise system and the franchisee.** This profile predicts both franchise fit and performance! This, in turn, saves everyone precious time, money and pain. Again, this is just one of the many tools I use in my process, but it is a valuable one. I can't tell you how many times my candidates have taken the Zorakle and remarked, "OMG, that's me!"

Ok, back to where we were. Once I review all of the information and make note of items we should discuss, I will offer you a no-commitment, complimentary consultation. If you feel that our personalities align and you like what you've learned about me, you accept, and we schedule a virtual meeting.

You are only agreeing to one thing: you are excited to learn more and are willing to put in the time to work with me on a weekly basis. You agree to follow my process.

After 10 years of working in this business, I have streamlined my process to cross all the T's and dot all the I's before I present brands for you to consider. I don't just throw "sh__" on a wall, as they say. There is a reason why I choose each brand I show you, but to do that, I need to make sure I totally "get" what you are looking to do and "why."

This is why I developed what I call my "consultation interview." I want to learn who you are…. what makes you tick…and what you are looking to gain by investing in a franchise.

In fact, this part of the process is the most rewarding and memorable for me. When I think back to the many women candidates I have worked with over the years, I am intrigued by their diverse stories, backgrounds, and reasons for wanting to become a business owner. And maybe even more importantly, I remember all those who ultimately chose not to pursue franchising as an option to achieve their goals. The "why not" became a focal point of my desire to help women and what ultimately became the catalyst for this book.

I need to learn who you are so that I can put myself in your shoes when choosing brands to present to you. As I am sure you understand by now, I am passionate about ensuring that everyone who is interested in creating the life they love has the opportunity to do so. That being said, it is in your best interest that I explore every option. While you may *think* you know what type of business you are interested in, having years of experience in franchising, I have learned to spot interests, likes, and dislikes that you may not have recognized in yourself or that you considered sharing with me.

Let me give you an example. I was working with a client to find the best franchise for her based on her interests. She had shared with me during our consultation call and interviews that she "loves" dogs, so she was leaning toward a business that involved furry friends. After doing my due diligence and applying what I know about her, I understood that although she is passionate about dogs, is a dog business the best investment for her? In the end, I presented her with various options that I thought would be a better match for her financial needs, scheduling requirements, and management style.

So, let's look at some of the areas I evaluate during our consultation call to paint the big picture to help me identify some brands that may be appropriate for you:

Franchising may not be your first go-to when it comes to entrepreneurship and frankly, not many people are aware of the benefits and details of franchising. So, during our initial conversations, I will provide a nice overview of the elements of franchising, all the parts that make up the franchisor, and how the relationship between franchisor and franchisee works. I want to make sure you understand the components of the investment and ongoing fees so you understand the value of investing in the brand.

Going back to one of my initial questions, we have to talk about your 'why'! Why are you interested in becoming an entrepreneur or pursuing franchising as a business option? I won't rehash this now but will refer you back to Chapter Two so you can review what brought you to this point in the first place.

But to summarize, what are your goals for your business venture? Are you looking for an investment as a temporary career but then a saleable asset in the future? Maybe you want a business that you can leave for your children or even work with your children now. The choice is yours but your why and goals are critical in the selection and decision-making process so we will return to them often.

Just as important as how you got here is knowing where you see yourself going. Where do you see your life in five or ten years from now?

Ask yourself:

1. Do you see yourself retired?

2. Geographically, where do you see yourself living?

3. How many hours do you see yourself working? This will help us evaluate brands based on the level of involvement required.

I will ask you about other business options you may have looked at already and what you have liked and disliked about each. Remember that I learn just as much from what you don't like as I do about what gets you excited.

Your family's history in business is also very important. If you have owned businesses in the past or your father has, for example, that's relevant. It means you appreciate the entrepreneurial spirit and know what kind of hard work goes into owning and operating a successful business.

As part of the discovery process, we are going to get a little personal. Don't forget that my goal is to find the best fit for you for this very important decision. It is in your best interest to be as transparent and upfront with me as possible. It will not serve either of us any good to be less than forthcoming.

Especially when it comes to your support system. Just as in any business opportunity, you will need the support of your family and loved ones to stand beside you in this endeavor. Now, I am not saying that they must be involved in the business with you (although that is a possibility) but you must have the support of those around you that make this a success. I realize that this may not necessarily be what you expected to hear from me but the reality is that all have met a few nay-sayers in our lifetime, and some more than others. So, I'll just leave it at that.

But to ensure you start on the right foot, if there are any people in your world who do not support this idea, we want to include them in the process from day one. We don't want you to get excited about a brand and spend weeks going through the discovery process only to have that person put the kibosh on it at the last minute. That's very disappointing to everyone: you, of course, and the brand who was excited about getting a fabulous new franchisee like you onboard! As for me, don't ever worry about me! My goal is to help you find whatever it is that is the best fit for your next chapter and I will say that over and over again.

We also want to talk about your lifestyle and, more specifically, your ideal lifestyle. What does your ideal lifestyle look like? Of course, that's a loaded question but, nevertheless, an important one. When you consider what your lifestyle will look like, consider some of the following questions:

- What hours do you want to work or be open?

- What is the level of involvement you would like to have? For example, an owner-operator with direct management of the business, a semi-absentee with a manager involved in the day-to-day, or an investor with no direct day-to-day involvement. One option may be to be semi-absentee now and transition to fully absentee upon retirement.

- Will you commute to a location and if so, what is the farthest distance you would like to travel?

Ultimately, you and I will discuss your ideal lifestyle and scale back from there as necessary based on available opportunities.

Lastly, although this is not a complete list of topics that we will discuss, what type of management style do you have and prefer? What is your experience with managing employees? Have you been in a leadership role before? What is your preference for the number of employees and whether they are skilled or unskilled labor?

Your responses to the questions posed to you here, as well as many others, will lay the foundation for what types of brands I will present to you as we move forward.

Franchise Options

But before we get to that point, I have another major question for you: What kind of business do you want to own and/or operate? While it may be too early to definitively answer the question since you may not yet be familiar enough with franchising and various brands, I recommend you begin thinking about this as we progress in the discovery process.

So, let's keep going.

When looking at franchises, we can divide the types of franchises into two major categories, retail or service, and then we can divide those two major categories into subcategories.

A retail franchise is typically a brick-and-mortar establishment with a product or service that consumers want and are willing to travel to a location to get it. In this case, there are various other considerations that we will factor into the identification and selection process.

For example, because a building or space is required, there will be a build-out with associated expenses and time required for ramp-up. The management style question will come into play here as you evaluate various brands requiring skilled or unskilled labor. For example, McDonald's will require unskilled labor but a Massage Envy franchise would require trained employees.

A retail franchise has the advantage of following a multi-unit concept. In other words, once you build one, it's easier to open numbers two and three. I worked with a candidate back in 2018 who was looking to open multiple units. His vision was that he would open unit number one, manage it himself to get a "boots on the ground" experience, and then turn it over to a manager when he opened number 2, and so on. This candidate ended up with an empire of 7 units!

A service business, on the other hand, is one in which customers hire you to come to them. There is typically no build-out required, so it can be home-based, making the ramp-up process and timing much quicker. This also typically means lower costs depending on whether equipment is needed or not.

Service businesses do typically require skilled laborers to provide the service and can be further divided into B2B and B2C. As an example of a business-to-business (B2B) model, think Abrakadoodle Art Enrichment or Crestcom Leadership Training. Tutor Doctor or Color World Painting are examples of business-to-consumer (B2C) model franchises.

If you are looking to have multiple units of a service business, consider purchasing multiple territories that can be conveniently operated from the same home office. I had a client back in 2018 who actually ended up purchasing two different franchises at the same time that were both children's enrichment concepts. His feeling was that he would have the same clients and parents for both businesses and could run them out of the same office. He could serve the community in an efficient, cost-effective way.

Financing

At some point, we must talk about money and finances. It's imperative that I know how much you are comfortable investing and what you need to make! Your responses to the questionnaires and forms will give me the parameters, but I really need to hear it from your mouth, where your comfort level is for investment, return on investment, and risk tolerance.

It is a very poor reflection on me as your consultant to introduce you to a brand that does not validate that you can reap the rewards you are seeking from franchise ownership. If you have $5 million in net worth but really are terrified to invest any more than $250K, then I absolutely need to know that. The great thing is that I can work within almost any parameter. Think about when you buy a house. You tell the realtor your range and they show you homes within that price range. What is the point in looking at a $3 million dollar home if you can't qualify for a loan that would allow you to not only buy that home but also pay the taxes and utilities on the home? It's the same with franchising. The franchise brands expect me to prequalify my candidates so that I am not showing them a brand they are not qualified for. I do not ever check or confirm anything you tell me, but it's an honor system.

There are many creative solutions to fund a franchise investment. I will refer you to a funding specialist who is an expert in working with franchises like the ones we will look at. This is what they do every day, all day long. Working with a funding specialist will help alleviate some of your fears and expand your viable options, helping you get on your way to franchise ownership.

Do I have your attention? Was this a fear holding you back that has now been alleviated?

I am super excited to share the next steps in the process with you, so let's keep going!

Key Takeaways:

In order to guide you toward living the life you love, I have to first know what that life looks like. Using the system I have developed over the course of my career, I will get to know who you are, what drives you, and how you see your life in the future.

I will educate you so that you can then make the decision that will certainly change the trajectory of your life as it did mine.

Use this space like a check list to make sure you have some of the documents and resources we will discuss during our consultation:

- *Resume*

- *LinkedIn profile*

- *Questionnaire*

Also, let's consider:

What are your goals for your business venture?

_____

_____

Are you looking for an investment as a temporary career but then a saleable asset in the future?

_____

_____

Do you want a business that you can leave for your children or even work with your children now?

_____

_____

Chapter 6:

Let Me Get To Work

———————— ～ ————————

To this point in the process, all of it has been about you, your preferences, goals, and motivations. However, this is a shared experience and I am personally invested in your success. My motivation is pure and simple: to help you create a life you will love.

That being said, I want you to be comfortable sharing with me and trust that I have your best interest at heart. The more you share with me in the consultation, the more I will really "get" you as a person and understand your goals.

The Fun Begins

During the next phase of the process, I will step away to conduct some research and compile a list of brands that I believe may be options for you. This sounds very simple but it's actually quite complicated. I will pull all of the tools we have put in my toolbox and lay them out in front of me to create a candidate profile. I then use this profile to start reviewing the hundreds of brands in our inventory to see which ones I think best reflect your intentions and fit the franchise culture you would work best in.

My work doesn't stop there. Next, I have to do territory checks with each brand to make sure that when I present the brand to you and get you all excited, the territory you are looking at is actually available. Nothing is more disappointing than when my clients have chosen their favorite brand, and then the territory is sold.

Last summer, we had the most unusual situation. A hot new brand hit the market and candidates were literally flocking to get in on it. I had multiple candidates go thru the process, but when it came time for "Meet the Team Day" (we will cover this soon), some of my candidates were finding out that when they got to this point, there was more than one candidate vying for the same territories and only one would get them. In all my years, I have never seen anything like this. I have vowed that this will never again happen to any of my candidates, so I must get the complete picture before I present a brand.

So, to reiterate, I will review the information you provided during our consultation, conduct a search of available and appropriate brands, and evaluate the cultural and business fit, looking to find a match for your preferences.

This is the point where I tell my candidates, you get to sit back and enjoy the ride now. When I was in your shoes, I was so excited to see what brands would be presented. I couldn't wait to see if there was going to be something shown that would get me excited! So get ready...here I come. I hope I present you with some expected types of brands but also some that are really outside your expectations. After all, that's my job: to find the brands that you would not have thought of on your own. I hope you have fun with this process. It's educational but it's all for a purpose. Each brand was selected for a reason and I will give you that reason as well as a high-level overview of the brand.

Timeline Expectations

You may be thinking that we have been moving pretty quickly through the process, and you would be right in most cases. The process from our initial conversation until you sign the franchise agreement typically takes between 60 and 90 days on average.

Now, while this does not seem like a long time, especially for making such a big decision, what else would you need to know? If there is anything else that you want to know about the process, the brand, financing, or expectations, all you have to do is ask.

I've had several clients who have gone through the entire process, gotten to the edge of the cliff, and decided not to take the leap. And that's ok too. But understand that by becoming a franchise owner, you are investing in yourself and your financial future, making it all the more important that it is a good fit.

I hope I have shared enough about my process to understand that franchising may not be for everyone. However, I will also share that of those who initially chose not to follow the path of franchising, most returned within a few months to complete the process.

I get it! Making big decisions like becoming an entrepreneur or making a large investment are major life decisions that should not be taken lightly. Remember the story I shared earlier of when a business I purchased was not a good fit? It can happen to anyone and you cannot foresee every situation or environment.

However, I assure you that we will do our due diligence together, and I will help you ensure that you are making the best decision for you and your life.

Let me ask you, what will happen differently in your life if you wait and make the decision next year or six months from now? Will the decision be any easier? Will the process be simpler? I believe in taking opportunities as they present themselves. If you are here now, reading this book, it means that a door is opening for you at this moment in time. Where will your life be in the next six months?

I'd also like you to consider how much you may be missing out on if you don't jump at this opportunity. Again, I understand that this decision could be the difference between where you are now and where you want to go, and for most of us, change is scary. But isn't it even scarier to think that if you don't make a move, you may not achieve your goals? For me, that thought is terrifying and is the catalyst that pushes me to continue moving forward.

The consultation call that I have just outlined, or gathering of information and really getting to know what makes you tick, is the most important step of MY process. I have to leave that call already excited that I GET you! I know what you are looking to do and my brain is already ticking with ideas of brands I can't wait to check territory on. This is where I get super excited to get to work and introduce you to brands.

So, how do you feel right now? Are you excited?

Get ready.......I'm about to get to work. For this next step, you get to sit back and let me present brands to you that could possibly help you achieve exactly what you are looking to do!

Key Takeaways:

As far as I am concerned, this is the most important step in the process. It is my time to take all that I have learned about you and what I know of the franchise industry and available brands and get to work finding the brands that will help you achieve your goals.

How are you feeling so far about the process?

_____

_____

_____

_____

Do you have any questions for me while I get to work on identifying brands that may be a good fit and will help you achieve your goals?

_____

_____

_____

_____

PART III -
THE DISCOVERY

You are now ready to dive into the most exhilarating part of the process—Discovery! By now, I have presented you with an array of brands that I believe could be options for you as a franchise owner. Because of our lengthy conversations and my diligence to get to know you, you should have the knowledge and tools you need to make sure you and the franchisor are a good fit.

But don't worry—I am not going anywhere! I will still be with you throughout the rest of your journey.

Let's get started!

Chapter 7:

Who Are They?

"Take time to get to know people. Understand where they are coming from, what is important to them. Make sure they are with you." ~ *Jack Welch*

―――――――◯◯◯――――――――

Meet the Brand

Are you excited? I have presented you with brands at a high level, and you have chosen which of the brands you'd like to learn more about. We have discussed together why these brands were chosen for you and why I think they fit within the parameters you have set. After our call, I have done what is called "registering you with the brand." This just means that I have let the brand know that I have presented their brand to you. This is a requirement of my job. I have attached a copy of some of the tools, such as the CQ, the Zorakle SpotOn! Profile and even possibly your resume. I want the brand to have a great idea of who you are before they schedule the introductory call with them. They will reach out via phone or email to schedule the first call. Remember at this point, you have not committed to anything except one call to learn more about the brand.

First calls or introductory calls are usually a one hour webinar presented by the brand representative. You will have one call for each brand. For that one brand. The brand representative or development person is a person who spends every day speaking to people just like you who are considering this franchise for themselves. Their entire days are spent taking folks like you through the process.

They know the brand inside and out and know what the franchisors are looking for. They know their culture, requirements, and area opportunities. You are in great hands with these people and in almost every case, I will have worked with them all before. I entrust them to my candidates and I do not take that lightly.

Let's look at some of the areas that will be covered by brand reps on most first calls.

Note: Many of the brands I present will follow the process I am describing to you, but some will have a slightly different approach since, like each of us as people, every brand is also slightly different.

On the introductory call, the representative will usually provide an outline of their process, including how long the process takes and when and if they have a deadline for a decision at the end of the process. They need to know that you can and are happy to follow a process. Remember that with franchising, you must be able to follow a set of predefined systems or processes in order to be successful. If you can't follow their system in the discovery process, how will you be as a franchisee?

They are looking to see if you are a fit for the brand as much as you are looking to see if this brand is a good fit for you. Here are some other topics that will be covered, most likely on the first call:

- What is the history of the franchise? The next area the brand rep will review with you is the history of the franchise. They will share the background of the people leading and handling development for the brand, how it got its start, and when they started franchising. You want to know how many units they've sold and where there is still availability and room for more growth.

- What is the brand's mission? What is the service or product and how does it matter to customers or how is it relevant to the community?

- Industry Insights. The presentation will often include industry insights to help you get a feel for the demand for the service or product you are considering here. For example, what is it that makes this brand a franchise? Is there a set curriculum or unique service that is being offered? This is the chance for the brand to show off and brag about the incredible business they have created.

- What business model does the franchise utilize? For example, who is the target customer, where is the product or service offered? What square footage is required for a brick-and-mortar establishment? How many different revenue streams are there?

- What technology does the brand utilize? They will talk about the technology the brand utilizes for CRM as well as for client tracking, quoting, etc. In many cases, technology can make the difference as to why not just anyone can do it on their own and sometimes, the investment in technology can be millions!

- Toward the end of the presentation, the brand representative will usually recap all of the highlights and also talk about the leadership team. They will explain the home office location and how the team supports you. Remember, don't fall in love with your brand rep because 9 times out of 10, he/she does not participate in the actual operations of the business, and you won't deal with them again after you join the brand. Once you commit to buying into the franchise, you will have the opportunity to meet the members of the leadership team who will actually support you in your day-to-day operations of the business.

- Lastly, the brand rep will hopefully ask you if you'd like to schedule the next call.

When you hear about this brand, do you get excited? Do you wish it was available in your town? Each time I learned about the brands I invested in, I immediately got excited and thought, "Wow, I would use this or would buy this!!" This is what I am most excited to hear at this point in the process. You still have a lot to learn about the brand, but if you are excited about learning more, then this brand is a keeper for now anyway.

Remember that I will be with you each step of the way. During a follow-up call, we will recap each of the first calls you've had, including all the things you like and dislike about each brand. This is where my value really comes in, as I help you navigate the entire process from start to finish.

Here is a recommendation I received from a brand rep I worked with. Casey Morris was the development person for CarePatrol. He wrote,

"Linda and I worked together on a prospective candidate who ultimately chose to join CarePatrol. Throughout the process, Linda was a fantastic partner-very communicative and helpful in providing the client the outside perspective and impartial advice for her to come to a confident and educated decision."

On our follow-up call, after you have had all of your introductory calls, I will ask you lots of questions. We will speak openly about what you liked and, again, just as importantly, what didn't you like. Sometimes, at this point, it may spark me to introduce another brand because learning what you do and don't like may remind me of another brand that I had as a backup. Most importantly, however, do you want to have a second call with the brand and continue learning? If yes, for at least one of the brands, let's keep going.

Unit Economics Call

The next step in the process is to have a unit economics call, which will help determine if this is a brand that can help you get to where you are going financially. Some brands will call it a unit economics call and others may just call it a financial review call. Whichever name they choose, this is the call where the brand representative will discuss in detail all of the fees, investment levels, and any earnings claims that the brand is making in the Franchise Disclosure Document, which I will discuss in greater detail in Chapter 9.

The key discussion on a unit economics call will be:

- Initial investment - What is the all-in cost range to open the first unit of this franchise? This may include the franchise fee, the equipment cost, the grand opening marketing budget, and many other items. This is all important because this is the first parameter people ask me about. "How much will this cost?"

- Ongoing fees - This discussion will surround items like the ongoing royalty and advertising fund fees but also ongoing monthly subscription fees for things like technology and customer relationship management software.

- Item 19 - The earnings claim that is shown in the FDD. This is the item where many prospects jump to when opening the FDD. Although brands may show their earnings claim in many formats, this is where they choose to disclose actual numbers that candidates can use to evaluate the earnings potential. For example, some brands may just show you the annual sales of their Top Quartile, Second Quartile, etc. Others may just show you the average sales ticket. It depends on the business type and the brand. This can certainly make it tricky because you may be comparing apples to oranges, but I will help you get the information you need for all brands.

- Cash Flow Projections - If you are lucky, your brand may set you up with a proforma or budget tool, that you can use to drop in numbers you gather from the FDD but also from your validation calls. See the example below.

MONTHLY ESTIMATED BUDGET	January
CONSULTATIONS	0
% OF CONVERSIONS CONSULTATION TO A PAYING CLIENT	0%
TOTAL CLIENTS	0
AVERAGE REVENUE PER CLIENT	$0
	January
GROSS REVENUE	$0
GROSS REVENUE FROM RETAIL	$0
TOTAL GROSS REVENUE	$ -
RENT(4)	$ -
MARKETING & PROMOTION(5)	$ -
REQUIRED SOFTWARE(6)	$ -
EXERBOTICS TECHNOLOGY FEE(7)	$ -
INSURANCE(8)	$ -
UTILITIES, PHONE, ISP(9)	$ -
WATER FILTRATION LEASE(10)	$ -
PAYROLL(11)	$ -
ROYALTIES	$ -
CREDIT CARD PROCESSING	$ -
TOTAL OF CERTAIN EXPENSES	$ -
	January
REVENUE - EXPENSES	$ -

Proformas like this can make all the difference in the world. It allows prospects to know what numbers they need to get during validation so they can create a meaningful budget. For clients who are numbers and data focused, I will strive to show you brands who are very transparent like this on their unit economics call.

Note: Remember that unless these numbers are disclosed in the FDD (Chapter 9), they are not privy to discuss them. In that case, you will have to wait until Validation to gather this information from current or past owners.

FDD Review Call

The FDD call with the brand rep is the first real review you will have of the brand's FDD. On this call, the brand rep will simply explain each of the disclosures in detail.

By this point, I will have already reviewed a generic FDD with you so you will know what to expect, and I will coach you ahead of time on what to look for on the call. I will have described for you what the 23 sections of the FDD contain and what to look for in each section. The brand representative's job is to clarify for you what their brand has chosen to declare in each section. You will know if you feel comfortable with their explanations. For example, if they try to tell you that 100 lawsuits are nothing to worry about or the 3 bankruptcies were not their fault, run for the hills as these would be a big fat red flag! However, if they explain that the reason they do not make an earnings claim in their Item 19 is because they have only been around for 2 years, then that makes perfect sense.

What you are hoping to learn on this call is a lot of valuable, transparent information that will help you make your decisions or at least give you a jumping-off point. The most important thing is to make notes of what is missing from this document so you will know what you will need to ask during the validation stage.

For example, if the franchise brand shows you a Profit and Loss statement from one or several of the franchisees, look at the expenses listed. Is there anything missing? Does it include a manager's salary, which is key if you are going to run this semi-absentee? If they only show corporate stores, are they adding a Royalty fee and Advertising fund fee like you would pay?

When the brand reviews the FDD with you, look closely at Item 7 and ask them questions. What is the reason between the high end of the investment and the low end? Does it make sense? Sometimes, the difference can be leasing equipment vs. purchasing. Sometimes, it's because the low end shows a home office, and the high end shows an executive suite outside the home. These are just examples of things to look for.

When they review item 20, which shows the units open, closed, transferred, etc., it's important to see a pattern of growth. If you don't see that pattern, ask the questions. You want transparent answers that make sense.

I could write an entire book on the FDD, but who would read it? At this point in the process, you are just looking to feel good about what you are seeing, with no red flags and lots of transparency. Now it's time to look at territory. You are now picturing your business, but where will it be?

Key Takeaways:

During this first part of the discovery process, there are so many exciting things that will happen:

- Introductory calls with brand representatives

- Unit economics call where you will learn about fees, investment levels, and any earnings claims

- FDD review call where you will receive valuable, transparent information that will help you make your decisions

Use this space to take some notes and keep track of questions during each call with brand representatives:

_____

_____

_____

_____

_____

_____

_____

_____

Chapter 8:

Territory and Mapping

"I do not know anyone who has got to the top without hard work. That is the recipe. It will not always get you to the top, but should get you pretty near." ~ Margaret Thatcher

───────〜───────

D on't worry; while it may seem that you will be having quite a few calls or webinars with each brand, early in the process, you will be thankful you did once it comes down to making a decision.

The Territory Question

In this next stage of the process, you will talk with each brand about territory and mapping. Why is this important? Franchisors define territories in order to protect the rights and investment of franchisees. Having defined territories ends any confusion as to where a franchisee can market and serve customers. It mitigates conflict between neighboring franchisees so they can actually work together without worrying about overlap.

Some franchises do not sell protected territories. I know of several service businesses that allow their franchisees to work anywhere in the country. Executive recruiting is an industry that works like this most times. With this said, however, many times, where you can market is defined to a territory.

Here's a good example of this. Let's say you have an "in" with a business in your local area but they have offices in three states. If you have built a relationship with that company, the brand wants you to be able to place executives at any of their locations.

During a mapping call with the brand, you may inquire as to what defines a territory and also what is and is not available in your desired location. The brand representative should explain what the demographics look like and what stipulates a single territory. For example, depending on the product or service, a territory may be defined by mileage, population size, or even road boundaries. If you don't know what a single looks like, how can you agree to multiple territories?

They should explain how the territory is protected as well as whether or not neighboring territories are sold and make sure to ask about the owners! Clear territory definitions and detailed maps can help avoid potential disputes in the future as a result of ambiguity.

At this point, I get really excited for each of my clients as a picture of what franchise ownership looks like begins to take shape. Can you feel the energy in the air?

Key Takeaways:

Having territories is often unique to franchising but is a very important component, requiring careful evaluation before you make a decision. As you can imagine, your territory, being the domain in which you can market and sell, can make or break your buying decision.

- *What territories are available to you?*

  _____

  _____

- *What territories interest you the most?*

  _____

  _____

- *What questions about territories come to mind?*

  _____

  _____

Chapter 9:

The All-Important

Franchise Disclosure Document (FDD)

—————————⁓—————————

D o not be afraid! The FDD is not that scary. The franchise disclosure document is a document that all franchisors in the US are required to file annually and provide to prospective franchisees. It is, however, an extensive document that provides information on the franchise system and franchisor. The purpose is to provide you, the potential franchisee, with detailed and transparent information about the franchisor's business, allowing you to make informed decisions before entering into a franchise agreement. Each FDD contains the same 23 sections or, as they are referred to, Items.

After you have had your introductory calls, and possibly even after your unit economics calls, the brand will provide you, usually electronically, a Franchise Disclosure Document. You will be required to provide a signature upon receipt, which does nothing but allow you to enter into an agreement after 14 days. It doesn't mean you have to ever enter into an agreement, but it prevents a franchisor from pressuring you into making a rash decision before then.

Here are a few key reasons why the FDD is important for validation when looking at franchises:

1. Background information – The FDD contains details about the franchisor's executives, litigation history, and other relevant background information. This helps potential franchisees assess the credibility and stability of the franchisor.

2. Transparency – The FDD provides comprehensive information about the franchisor's history, financial health, and the overall performance of the franchise system. This transparency helps potential franchisees understand what they are getting involved in.

3. Costs and fees – Items 5,6, and 7 outline the costs relating to becoming a franchisee and then operating as a franchisee. This information is crucial for assessing the financial feasibility of entering into a franchise agreement.

4. <u>Legal and contractual obligations</u> – Contractual obligations of both the franchisor and franchisee are clearly outlined in the FDD. This helps potential franchisees understand the terms and conditions of the franchise relationship.

5. <u>Performance data</u> – If a franchisor chooses to make an earnings claim, it would be outlined in Item 19. This data helps franchise candidates model out the potential financial profitability of the franchise.

6. <u>System Growth</u> – Item 20 will show how many new units have opened and how many, if any, have closed or were transferred. This is another area that will help potential franchisees see any patterns or areas of concern or growth.

During our time together, I will do an FDD overview call with you where I will discuss all 23 of these items with you. I want you to be prepared when your first brand sends over their FDD for you to review. As you move forward in your due diligence, you will view the FDD in detail with the brand development rep because they will know the ins and outs of their specific FDD. One of your final steps in the journey to franchise ownership may be an FDD review call with an established franchise attorney. He or she will make sure that before you sign any documents, you are completely comfortable with everything in the FDD and franchise agreement.

It may feel daunting when you first receive the FDD, but don't let it be. This whole process is designed to be a step-by-step process.

Key Takeaways:

Since this is such an important component of the process, it is worth again listing the key reasons why it is important to validate a franchise, which we will discuss in more detail in the next chapter.

1. Background information

2. Transparency

3. Costs and fees

4. Legal and contractual obligations

5. Performance Data

6. System growth

Be sure you are well-informed. What other questions come to mind as you review the FDD?

_____

_____

_____

_____

_____

_____

Chapter 10:

Validation and Meet the Team

B y now, you have probably learned a lot about franchising, various brands, and what you like and don't like. It is time to begin the next phase of the process, which includes validation calls with owners—which might be the most important step of the process!

Does It All Validate?

The validation process is taking what you learned during the discovery process and validating it. In other words, ensuring that you have a full picture of the franchise you are interested in buying into to protect your investment and help you to make a sound decision.

As part of the FDD, franchisors are required to provide a list of franchisees with whom you can have a direct conversation about the brand and their experiences. Of course, as with any "referral," it is common to only get those contacts who are guaranteed to provide a glowing reference or paint a beautiful experience. Although the franchisor is hopefully being honest and transparent, they only see the process from one perspective. And to make a good decision, you need to understand the process, culture, and market from a real-life, hands-on point of view.

So you want to speak with a cross-section of all types of franchisees—yes—even those who may not be very happy. So that you can make an informed decision, you need to see the brand from all perspectives and angles but yet understand that everyone will have a different experience based on their individual situations. You want to speak to franchisees, including top performers, those who are new to the franchise, and maybe even those who were not successful.

When talking with other franchisees, you have to know how to read between the lines of what a franchisee is telling you and decipher as much from what they are not saying as much as what they do.

Here are a few questions I recommend asking franchise owners when I am considering a brand.

Note: I also recommend asking the same questions to each of the franchisees you speak to so you can get a complete picture of the brand (360 degree-view) as well as any trends or tendencies that may emerge.

- What was your background before purchasing a franchise?

- What was your expected level of involvement?

- What were your goals or reason for buying a franchise (is it the same as yours?)

- Were you satisfied with the onboarding process and support you received when you started?

- Has franchise ownership met your expectations?

- Why did you select this particular brand?

- Are you interested in buying additional territories?

Validation is your opportunity to obtain first-hand information from current owners and/or those who have left the system and to understand why, or maybe more importantly, why not, this brand was a good choice for them (and possibly you!) While the FDD will disclose a good amount of detail, there is nothing more important in making a decision, especially one of this magnitude, than speaking to people with feet on the street.

Now, I would be remiss if I didn't remind you that the information you receive during a validation call is, of course, a franchisee's opinion and experiences. I caution you to take the information you receive from each person with a grain of salt, not allowing one particular experience to sway you one way or the other.

The validation process is useful in helping you make an informed decision but it also is a way for brands to vet potential candidates. Franchisees you speak with may report back to corporate with feedback about you and your potential fit as a franchise owner. It is important always to be polite, respectful, and have an abundance mindset, demonstrating your desire to be a part of the team and, most importantly, be the real you. As we've discussed before, a major part of this entire process is being true to yourself.

On the other hand, when you are on validation calls, it is okay to ask questions, and it is highly recommended since franchisors also want to be confident that you did your due diligence in making the right decision.

On to Meet the Team Day, where you get to do an on-site visit, meet the corporate team leadership, and see a product or facility at work!

Meet the Team Day

Considered the final step in the process, Meet the Team Day is an important component of your overall discovery and evaluation of a brand. Typically, this step occurs by invitation only once a franchisor has deemed you a fit and is ultimately a mutual interview process. In other words, you are there to showcase yourself as prepared and confident as a potential franchisee representing their brand. It is a chance for the franchisor to evaluate the risk that they are about to take in partnering with *you*.

It is also an opportunity for you to meet the leadership team and learn more about the corporate culture. Again, as I've mentioned throughout, this business opportunity must be a good fit for both parties.

Typically, a Meet the Team event includes a dinner out to get to know one another on a more casual basis, then a day of presentations by various departments, including finance, marketing, and business operations. The agenda will more than likely conclude with a tour of the facility and/or operations.

In my experience, 80% of candidates leave a Meet the Team day and go on to purchase the franchise. This is a good indicator that this final step is just the thing both parties need to seal the deal.

Now, don't let this step scare you. You knew it was inevitable that if you were pursuing a franchise opportunity, at some point, you would have to meet the folks who make it all happen. This should not deter you from moving forward but rather reassure you that you are stepping into an environment that is supportive and that your success is of paramount importance to the brand. Besides, I will be there every step of the way to coach and guide you and even provide a little hand-holding along the way.

And now that you have completed each of the steps, time is up!

Key Takeaways:

Validation is your opportunity to obtain first-hand information from current owners and/or those who have left the system and to understand why, or maybe more importantly, why not, this brand was a good choice for them (and possibly you!)

This business opportunity must be a good fit for both parties.

Use this space to take notes and answers to some of the following questions during the validation stage:

- *What was your background before purchasing a franchise?*

  _____

  _____

  _____

  _____

- *What was your expected level of involvement?*

  _____

  _____

  _____

  _____

- *What were your goals or reason for buying a franchise (is it the same as yours?)*

_____

_____

_____

_____

- *Were you satisfied with the onboarding process and support you received when you started?*

_____

_____

_____

_____

- *Has franchise ownership met your expectations?*

_____

_____

_____

_____

- *Why did you select this particular brand?*

_____

_____

_____

_____

- *Are you interested in buying additional territories?*

_____

_____

_____

_____

Chapter 11:

The Time Is Up

"Nothing is more difficult and therefore more precious than to be able to decide." ~ Napolean Bonaparte

---~---

It's Decision Day!

The last step in the process you have been following is **to make your decision**. This may be a formal meeting with the brand representative, or it may just be that a deadline was set. Either way, at this point, there is no more for you to learn, and it's about "holding your nose and jumping in." It's the time to have faith that you are ready for change. It should feel scary and yet exciting all at one time. I always tell my clients to remember that a rush of adrenaline feels the same for fear as excitement. You and only you can choose which one to go with.

A certain amount of fear is expected with change. It's part of the normal human experience. Change, despite its challenges, offers opportunities for growth. Back in Chapter 2, we discussed the reasons you are here reading this book. If you didn't want change, you wouldn't be here.

Facing and overcoming fear or anxiety can lead to new skills, perspectives, and achievements.

How can you lessen the fear and anxiety? Simple......by reflecting on all the hard work you have put into this process. Recognize that you have done your homework. You have learned about the franchise. You have visited the home office and met the leadership team either in person or virtually. You have spoken to other owners who have validated what you have learned. You feel comfortable with your projections for the business, both financial and operational.

You are ready to make this decision!

Do you still need more encouragement? Let's discuss the franchise agreement.

After you make your decision, and if that decision is to move forward, please remember that YOU ARE NOT LEGALLY BOUND AT THIS POINT! You are simply telling the brand that your intent is to move forward. You will still have time and I will always recommend that you hire a franchise attorney to do a legal review of the agreement. So take a cleansing breath, and let's learn what that's all about.

What is Decision Day? It can mean many things depending on where you are in life. In fact, isn't every day a decision day where we are faced with multiple decisions, each with the possibility of impacting tomorrow?

In terms of making an investment in your future, Decision Day is the day on which you choose to move forward with one of the brands I presented and which you have vetted. It is the day that will mark a new beginning for you and your family.

Decision Day marks the line drawn in the sand between where you are and where you are going.

To help you make the all-important decisions to proceed as a franchise owner, and before you commit, I want to review some questions to ask yourself to ensure you fully understand the following five items:

1. **Territory:** Do you fully understand the territory you will be responsible for? Is it exclusive, or will others be operating in your territory as well? If there are definitive zipcodes or parameters, make sure you are clear on your borders. Also, make sure you are clear on whether or not those borders restrict you on marketing as well as operating. Remember, bigger is not always better.

2. **Fees:** Review Item 6 and Item 7 in the FDD. Make sure you are clear on the ongoing fees you will be required to pay, such as royalties or ad fund fees, as well as all upfront fees, like the franchise fee or training fees. Be clear as to who the fees are paid to and when.

3. **Vendors:** Many franchisors require you to purchase supplies and materials from specified vendors they have negotiated special rates with. Be clear on which supplies or services have required vendors.

4. **Franchise Term:** Be clear as to the initial term of your franchise agreement and the requirements for renewal. The last

thing you want to do is build a viable business only to find you are not eligible for renewal because you did not meet the terms.

5. **Termination:** Be clear on the terms for voluntary and involuntary termination by both you as well as the franchisor. All requirements should be spelled out clearly under each scenario. Also, make sure you are clear as to the different requirements upon termination due to the transfer or sale of your franchise. Many times, they are different.

How do you feel? Nervous, I am sure....that is normal. But it is time to get excited as you move onto the legal review...the last step before finalizing your agreements and making your dreams become a reality!

The Legal Review

"The greatest things in life all require commitment, sacrifice, some struggle and hardship. It's not easy but absolutely worth it." ~ Robin S. Sharma

So you have told the brand that you are moving forward and you are excited but still a little uneasy. That's totally natural, as we discussed in the last chapter. I have told clients in the past that I'd be concerned if they weren't. It's a big commitment and a big decision! Let's talk about what a legal review is and is not.

When purchasing a franchise, a legal review is a crucial step to ensure that you fully understand the terms, obligations, and risks associated with the franchise agreement.

Remember that although the FDD outlines all the terms of the agreement, the actual Franchise Agreement is what you sign.

What a legal review is not is a revision of the FDD. Franchisors will not alter the FDD 99% of the time because if they did, they would have to disclose this in all future FDDs. This is good and bad. The good news here is that you wouldn't want to be at the annual conference and find out that the gal across from you got preferential terms to yours. You want to be in the same shoes as everyone who signed at the time you did. The bad news is, of course, that you probably won't get changes made that you may want unless they are immaterial.

The FDD is the core document that clarifies fees, territorial rights, training and support, duration of the agreement, renewal options, and termination clauses. A legal review will help you understand the implications of each clause and how they may impact your rights and responsibilities. The franchise agreement is the contract written using all of the terms in the FDD.

Here are some key aspects that are typically covered in a legal review:

- The legal review should delve into the financial aspects of the franchise, including initial franchise fees, ongoing royalty fees, advertising fees, and any other financial commitments. Understanding the financial obligations is crucial for budgeting and long-term planning.

- The review should clarify the territorial rights you will have. Ensure that the franchise agreement clearly defines your territorial rights and restrictions. Understand whether you have exclusive rights to a specific geographic area and the implications of any limitations on territorial exclusivity.

- The franchise may involve the use of trademarks, trade secrets, and other intellectual property owned by the franchisor. A legal review should cover how these intellectual property rights are licensed to you and any restrictions on their use.

- The level of training and support provided by the franchisor is typically outlined in the agreement. A legal review can help you understand the extent of the support, the costs involved, and any expectations regarding your performance.

- Review the terms related to the renewal of the franchise agreement and the conditions under which either party can terminate the agreement.Understanding these terms is essential for planning your long-term involvement with the franchise.

- Examine the dispute resolution mechanisms outlined in the agreement, including whether disputes are resolved through arbitration or litigation and the governing law.

- Ensure that the franchise agreement complies with relevant local, state, and federal laws. A legal review can help identify any clauses that may be unenforceable or conflict with legal requirements.

Now the question becomes, who should you use for this legal review? It is advisable to seek the assistance of an experienced franchise attorney who specializes in franchise law to conduct the legal review. They can provide valuable insights, explain legal terms, and ensure that you make an informed decision before entering into a franchise agreement.

I cannot stress enough the importance of the attorney being a franchise attorney and not just your family attorney. The franchise attorneys my candidates have used are familiar with not only the FDD and all of its sections, but in many cases, they have worked with the exact same brand you are looking at before. This means they know the franchisor; they have seen what areas the franchisor has been flexible with and, most importantly, where they have made concessions. A franchisor will never give a potential franchisee any rights that are materially different from any other franchisee, but sometimes, there are areas where they can make small accommodations. It can't hurt to try!

Within 48 hours, most franchise attorneys will turn around your legal review. You will have a Zoom call with them in most cases and go through the review section by section to make sure you are clear with everything and anything they highlighted. This is when you and the attorney will discuss any areas that need clarification or potential modification. You will want to get these back to the franchisor as soon as possible to stay within the signing deadline.

Here is a description of what a franchise attorney that I refer to often offers my clients. I receive nothing for this referral other than knowing they are in good hands.

HOUSTON BARNES

https://www.barneslaw.com/

1. A call to take the time to learn about you, your goals, and why you are choosing this particular franchise.

2. Comprehensive review of the Franchise Disclosure Document (FDD), the Agreement you will sign with the Franchisor, and all of its Exhibits.

3. Comprehensive written analysis of your Franchise Documents, including Indication of major red flags and critical provisions in the contract client may want to negotiate or consider further

4. Overview and outline of critical provisions in the contract, the client may want to negotiate or consider further, and potential strategies for such.

5. Phone/Zoom consultation (however long it takes- typically 30 min to 1 hour) with the Client regarding all the above.

6. Drafting of the language of an addendum if changes are negotiated with the franchisor.

(basically, everything to get you to the signing of the Franchise Agreement)

When you receive the final comments and any changes back from the franchisor you should feel good and be ready to finalize!

IT'S SIGNING TIME!

Let's Celebrate - It's Signing Day!

You are just one step away from fulfilling your dreams, achieving your goals, and creating the life you want to live.

This is the place where all the work is complete and there is only one possible thing that could be holding you back...fear!

Let's recap: You have defined and explained to me how you envision your life to be, where you see yourself going, and what you expect out of life. Why back down now, especially when you are this close?

I assure you that whatever doubts you are feeling or limiting beliefs that have held you back before, you are not alone. Everyone has felt those at one point or another. The question is, what are you going to do about it?

You have worked this hard, dreamt this big, and learned too much to turn back now! And don't forget that I am walking side by side with you. Imagine how you would feel if you had come this far and turned away this opportunity.

What would you tell your children if you gave up just before this last step in your journey to becoming a franchisee, signing the franchise agreement?

The franchise agreement is the document that defines the relationship between you and the franchisor. I like to think of it as a partnership agreement. It is a binding agreement, and although it may be daunting, know that its purpose is as much to protect you as it is for the franchisor. It is not meant to scare you away but rather provide you with another level of assurance that your life is moving in the right direction and that, with this one step, you will change the lives of others around you.

While it may seem that some of the information provided in this document is the same as that included in the FDD, don't worry. It will all become clear once we review it together.

When my clients reach Signing Day, I am always so proud of their accomplishments and the hard work they have put in.

And as you can see from the many satisfied franchisees I have worked with, it is always a joyous occasion for everyone!

Key Takeaways:

Decision Day is scary, nerve-wracking, and exhausting as you finally make the decision to take that leap of faith. But knowing that you are deciding TODAY to change your life for TOMORROW should be the best feeling ever.

But of course, there is still the legal review which cannot be sidestepped.

Lastly, it is time to put pen to paper and then celebrate your decision!

Decision Day is a time to celebrate!! Give yourself a huge round of applause for making this awesome decision to take your life to the next level!!!

_____

_____

_____

_____

_____

_____

_____

Conclusion

"We all have our own life to pursue, our own kind of dream to be weaving, and we all have the power to make wishes come true, as long as we keep believing." ~ Louisa May Alcott

"The purpose of life is to live it, to taste experience to the utmost, to reach out eagerly and without fear for new and richer experience." ~ Eleanor Roosevelt

―――――――⌐⌐―――――――

Although the word "conclusion" is typical for ending a book of this nature, I hesitate to use it as I, in fact, close out this journey. I believe wholeheartedly that although I have finished the last chapter on paper, this is only the beginning of a new chapter for you. As cliche as it may sound, and to reiterate Eleanor Roosevelt's profound words, "The purpose of life is to live it…"

I want to bring you back to my opening statement in which I said, "We must reach out, take risks, and step outside of our comfort zone so that we may experience life."

I have written this book specifically for women because as we find ourselves in various stages of our lives, times of transition, many of us stop searching for our purpose or settle for what others may want for us. I want all the best for myself and for YOU!

No one knows what the future holds, so I want to grab hold with both hands, *"reaching out eagerly and without fear for new and richer experiences!"*

From one woman to another, it is time to invest in yourself and pursue your dreams!

You only have one life to live, so it's time to take that risk!

If, at this point, you cannot picture yourself *not* becoming a franchise owner, reach out to me at **Freedom Franchise Advisors** to connect.

Epilogue

I f you weren't convinced yet that franchising is a business opportunity to help you achieve your goals and live the life you love, let me share some current trends and statistics about the industry.

What's Trending in Franchising?

The last several years have posed challenges that no one could have seen coming. From the COVID-19 pandemic to political unrest and division to an economic downturn. Yet, despite all of the unpredictability, we have survived! We have risen up from the devastation and for some people, the financial ruin of the last few years.

This reminds me that just because you experience bumps in the road or may not be where you want to be right "now," it does *not* mean that you are not meant to live the life you love at all. Life throws wrenches, buckets and viruses that intend to derail us for our dreams but I stand firm on the premise that if you know who you are, you can grab hold of the life you want.

Although your journey may have not been what you envisioned, it is never too late to become a business owner. And the statistics are out that demonstrate that franchising as a business option is not only viable for many women but can certainly be a lucrative and worthy endeavor.

Let's look at some of the recent facts and projected trends according to the International Franchise Association's (IFA) *2024 Franchising Economic Outlook* report:

- Franchising exceeded projections for 2023, with establishments estimated to have grown by 2.2% compared to the 1.9% previously forecasted thanks to increased interest rates and strong consumer spending.

- To further control inflation, it is expected that the Federal Reserve will reduce interest rates, making the cost of borrowing for prospective franchisees more affordable, thereby increasing franchise ownership by 1.9%.

- An additional 221,000 jobs are expected to be created with new franchise ownership in the United States alone in 2024.

- Total revenue generated by franchises is expected to increase more than $545 billion.

- The highest growth is expected to be realized in the personal services and quick service restaurant industries.

If you're considering becoming a business owner or entrepreneur, the statistics are clear: there are abundant opportunities for you. Throughout this book, I've emphasized that there's a franchise to match every lifestyle, preference, and requirement. The challenge is to identify the franchise brand that aligns perfectly with your goals, and I'm here to assist you with that.

I've enjoyed sharing the proces and look forward to getting to know you.

About the Author

———~———

L inda Schaeffer has been a franchise owner three times in her life, placing her in the shoes of a prospective franchise owner. Being a business owner while raising a family was the exact work-life balance Linda was looking for, and having the ability to involve her children in her businesses was amazing. She never once regretted her decision to move forward.

As a top-producing franchisee, Linda has a unique perspective when assisting those looking into franchise ownership. She prides herself on building and maintaining strong personal relationships with those who are serious about investigating real opportunities and understands the importance of communication and support throughout the candidate's journey.

Before entering the world of franchising in the 1990s, Linda spent years as a Certified Public Accountant assisting small businesses in maximizing profits and achieving success. In 2014, Linda founded her company, **Freedom Franchise Advisors**, to help people achieve their work-life goals as she did through franchise ownership.

In addition to her consulting, Linda has worked in franchise development for three major franchisors: Abrakadoodle, Crestcom, and MRINetwork. Having been on all sides of the equation, Linda has real knowledge of what it takes to be successful as a franchise owner.

Linda attended Babson College in Wellesley, MA as well as Rider University in Lawrenceville, NJ, where she graduated with a Bachelor of Science in Commerce with a major in Accounting.

Linda resides in Sarasota, Florida with her husband of 38 years, Scott. They enjoy spending their summers in Stone Harbor, New Jersey with their three children, Kevin (Daisey), Samantha (Zach), and Matt, and their four grandchildren, Lily, Emma, Scott, and Charlie.

References

1.   Author, N. (2015, January 14). Chapter 1: Women in Leadership. Pew Research Center. https://www.pewresearch.org/social-trends/2015/01/14/chapter-1-women-in-leadership/#:~:text=In%201965%2C%2039%25%20of%20women,47%25%20in%20November%202014).

2.   Women's small business ownership and entrepreneurship ... (n.d.-a). https://www.sbc.senate.gov/public/_cache/files/b/9/b99ffab8-b62a-48e1-95ba-b14c5451880b/D779F6653743546214AD6E09EAED29F7.women-entrepreneurship-report.pdf

3.   Kaufman, S. (2022, June 7). Council post: Why building relationships is essential to business success. Forbes. https://www.forbes.com/sites/forbesbusinesscouncil/2022/06/06/why-building-relationships-is-essential-to-business-success/?sh=5c63918c4b59

4.   Team, Z. E. (2021, February 18). Data report: Why Americans aren't starting businesses. Zapier. https://zapier.com/blog/potential-entrepreneurs-report/